HORNED ANIMALS

Written by NATHAN AASENG
Illustrated by ALCUIN C. DORNISCH

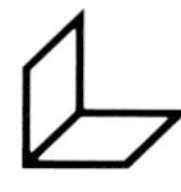

LERNER PUBLICATIONS COMPANY
MINNEAPOLIS, MINNESOTA

A NOTE ABOUT THE MEASUREMENTS IN THIS BOOK

In comparison to the animals on page 48, the boy is 4 feet (120 cm) and the woman is 5½ feet (165 cm) tall.

To Mikhaila

AN EARLY NATURE PICTURE BOOK

Library of Congress Cataloging-in-Publication Data

Aaseng, Nathan.
Horned animals.

(An Early nature picture book)
Summary: Describes the characteristics of several horned animals and explains the ways in which they use their headgear in courtship and battle.
1. Ungulata—Juvenile literature. 2. Deer—Juvenile literature. 3. Goats—Juvenile literature. 4. Horns—Juvenile literature. [1. Ungulates. 2. Horns] I. Dornisch, Alcuin C., ill. II. Title. III. Series.
QL737.U5A23 1987 599.73′5 87-4227
ISBN 0-8225-1119-3 (lib. bdg.)

Manufactured in the United States of America

2 3 4 5 6 7 8 9 10 96 95 94 93 92 91 90 89 88

CONTENTS

Have you noticed how many different kinds of wild animals have horns or antlers? Goats, buffalo, antelopes, oxen, and deer all grow sharp objects on their heads. For a long time, people have tried to find out why these animals have horns and antlers.

At first we might think they are weapons. Some of them look very much like swords or knives. Certainly when goats or bison fight with other animals, they lower their heads to aim those sharp points at their enemy. But if horns are meant to be weapons, they seem to be poor ones. Deer and antelopes have a much better chance of living if they run away from enemies than if they stand and fight. And can you think of an animal that uses horns or antlers to kill the food it needs? There is not a single one. Horns and antlers are worn only by plant-eaters. Animals that need to kill other animals for food must have different weapons.

The main reason for antlers and horns is to help the animals win contests. The most important contest among animals of the same kind, or **species**, is over mating rights. Every year, males fight each other over which will get to mate with the females to produce families. These contests are fought with the animals' heads. A good set of horns or antlers makes it possible for an animal to win. If an animal has especially big horns or antlers, it does not even have to fight. Other males are scared and give up without a battle.

For some animals, contests take place over feeding grounds. If one group of animals crowds in on another group, fights may break out. Again, horns and antlers come in handy for these fights. Among animals that fight often, females as well as males have antlers or horns.

There is a big difference between antlers and horns. Antlers are bones that grow each spring and fall off each autumn after mating season is over. During the summer, the tender bones are protected with a covering of soft, furry skin, or **velvet**. When the antlers harden, the velvet comes off in strips, and the animals are ready to battle during mating season. Horns, however, are just like hair or fingernails. They grow out of an animal's skin throughout its entire life. Unlike antlers, they do not fall off unless they are broken off.

Horns and antlers can be found in many sizes and shapes. The antlers of a bull moose may weigh 80 pounds (36 kg). Antlers belonging to other members of the deer family may weigh only a few ounces. Bighorn rams grow 30-pound (14-kg) horns that circle the animal's ears. A bison's horns, on the other hand, do little more than decorate its massive head. The horns of the Rocky Mountain goat (page 5) are short and plain. Other animals, like the blackbuck and ibex, have horns that bend and twist into beautiful designs. But no matter what they look like, horns and antlers help animals to win contests with other animals of the same species.

WHITE-TAILED DEER

Human hunters have nearly wiped out many of our most beautiful large animals. But they have not threatened the growing numbers of white-tailed deer. The white-tailed deer has become the most common large animal in North America. Over 12 million of them live in the United States alone.

Most of the white-tailed deer's natural enemies such as wolves and bears have been killed off. Because of this, the numbers of deer often grow too quickly. Then there are no longer enough twigs, leaves, and bark for all the deer in a certain area. In the winter, when food is scarce, many deer starve to death.

White-tailed deer are so good at hiding that it is difficult to believe there are so many of them around. They are large animals, standing over four feet (120 cm) high at the shoulder and weighing up to 300 pounds (135 kg).

Yet even when the leaves have fallen from the trees, you can walk through a forest full of deer and never see one. If you do come across a deer, you had better look quickly. Deer are easily startled and can run up to 30 miles (48 km) per hour for several miles.

Fawns, or baby deer, are even harder to see than their parents as their spotted coats blend in well with grass cover. **Does**, or female deer, keep their babies out of smell as well as out of sight. They constantly lick the fawns to keep them free of any smell that would attract a hungry enemy.

Only the male deer, known as **bucks**, grow antlers. Each spring, the bucks sprout a new set of antlers, which takes about four months to grow. Some people think that the age of a deer is the same as the number of points on its antlers. This is not true. But it is a fact that older deer usually grow bigger antlers. During the autumn mating season, bucks challenge each other for the right to mate with does. Sometimes, one buck backs away immediately from another buck with larger antlers. Other times, the bucks duel with their antlers for hours until one gives up. When winter arrives and mating season has ended, the antlers are no longer needed, so they drop off. If the buck lives through another tough winter, a new set will start to grow in the spring.

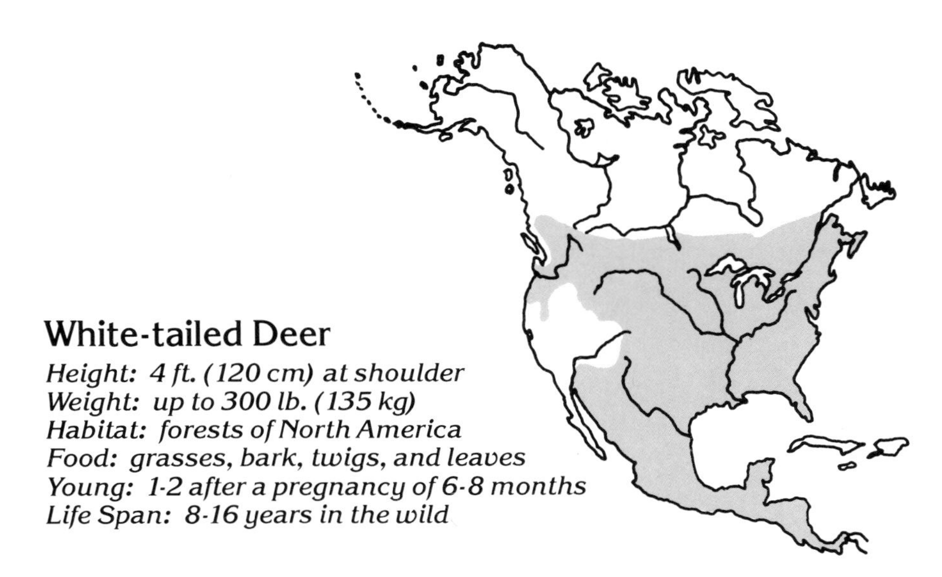

White-tailed Deer

Height: *4 ft. (120 cm) at shoulder*
Weight: *up to 300 lb. (135 kg)*
Habitat: *forests of North America*
Food: *grasses, bark, twigs, and leaves*
Young: *1-2 after a pregnancy of 6-8 months*
Life Span: *8-16 years in the wild*

CARIBOU

The stories of Santa Claus make it easy to remember that a species of deer called reindeer make their home near the North Pole. These animals with splendid antlers live in tamed herds in northern Norway, Sweden, and Finland. In North America, however, the same species of deer is called caribou.

The caribou of northern Canada and Greenland have never been tamed. Instead, they run wild through the **tundra**, the northern plains where it is too cold for trees to live. During the summers, caribou feed on grasses and shrubs of the tundra. But in the autumn, the caribou gather in huge herds and travel south, or **migrate**. Winters are so harsh on the northern tundra that even the rugged caribou must migrate each autumn in search of milder weather.

Caribou may travel as far as 800 miles (1,280 km) to the south each autumn. Even so, they live so far north that they cannot escape the cold. When they are caught in blizzards, caribou nestle down in the snow to keep out of the wind. Their wide hooves help them walk through the deep snow and clear feeding holes, and the sharp edges on their hooves keep them from sliding on frozen ground and ice.

Caribou feed on many kinds of trees and grasses. In the winter, they eat a brittle type of moss called **lichen**, which can be found growing on bare ground and rocks. Caribou eat one kind of lichen so much that the plant is called **reindeer moss**. Once a caribou has eaten a patch of reindeer moss, the plant will not grow back for nearly 10 years.

In the spring, the caribou take turns migrating southward. First, the females, or **cows**, return and give birth to their young. A few weeks later, the males, or **bulls**, and **yearlings**, one year old caribou, rejoin them.

Caribou shed parts of their outer covering throughout much of the year. When spring arrives, some of their thick winter fur falls out. Both males and females grow antlers, which are coated with velvet to nourish the growing bones. This velvet is shed painlessly when the antlers are fully grown. After the autumn mating season, the bulls' antlers fall off. The cows grow smaller and thinner antlers late in the summer. In June, the cows shed their antlers too.

Caribou

Height: *4-5 ft. (120-150 cm) at shoulder*
Weight: *240-700 lb. (108-315 kg)*
Habitat: *tundra, forests, and mountains of the Arctic*
Food: *grasses, plants, and lichen*
Young: *1 after a pregnancy of 8 months*
Life Span: *15 years in the wild*

MOOSE

The animal known in North America as the moose is called an elk in Europe. Like cattle and caribou, male moose are called bulls. Female moose are called cows, and the young are known as **calves**. But, in fact, these bulb-snouted creatures are the largest members of the deer family.

Few events in nature are more impressive than a battle between two bull moose for mating rights. These giants of the north woods can measure seven feet (210 cm) at the shoulders and weigh up to 1,800 pounds (810 kg). They carry huge antlers that stretch four to six feet (120 to 180 cm) across. Bull moose grow antlers during the summer. The velvet peels off the hardened antlers before they are used during the autumn mating season. When moose charge at each other with their huge antlers, they mean business! Sometimes they fight to the death.

Moose are well equipped to defend themselves. Such large, spreading antlers atop a powerful animal will scare away most other creatures. A moose can detect those that are not scared off with its keen senses of smell and hearing. Despite its size, a moose can sprint as fast as a deer when threatened. With all this protection, a healthy adult moose has little to fear from meat-eaters such as wolves or bears. Moose calves, however, make tempting targets for meat-eaters. Even though the cows defend their calves fiercely, few of the young animals survive to adulthood.

When watching a moose eat, you might think that nature has played a joke on it. The poor animal's legs are too long for its head to reach the ground. If the moose wants to eat ground plants or drink from a stream, it must kneel down or spread its front legs like a giraffe. But the long legs do help the moose step over logs and wade through soggy marshlands. They also make it possible for the animal to walk easily through deep snowdrifts in winter.

Moose do not always have to bend to get food and water, however, as leaves and bark from tree branches provide a meal within easy reach. During the warmer seasons, moose like to wade into lakes and ponds. This brings floating plants and drinking water closer to their mouths. We do not often think of moose as creatures of the water. But they even enjoy diving completely under the water to grab the juicy stems and roots of the water lily.

Moose

Height: 5½-7 ft. (165-210 cm) at shoulder
Weight: 500-1,800 lb. (225-810 kg)
Habitat: forests of North America
Food: bark, twigs, leaves, shrubs, and water plants
Young: 1-2 after a pregnancy of 8 months
Life Span: 15-20 years in the wild

BISON

That bearded, woolly-headed North American animal with the humped back is not a buffalo. It is really a bison. Buffalo live in Africa and Asia. They have fewer ribs than bison and do not have humps.

Although the bison population is slowly growing, the animal is still a symbol of shame to wildlife lovers. Before European settlers spread into the western plains of the United States, 50 million bison lived there in great herds. They wandered throughout the open plains, always searching for new grasslands. Native Americans, as well as wolves and bears, depended on bison for their food.

But white hunters began **slaughtering** the animals, killing hundreds of them, often just for the fun of it. By 1889, fewer than 600 remained. Just before it was too late, bison were protected by the U.S. government from any further killing. Even now, the animals can no longer roam freely.

Instead, they are kept in game preserves, where they can be cared for and protected.

Like other horned animals, bison have a extra stomach that helps to digest food. During the morning and evening, they bite off and swallow as much grass as they can. Then, while they are resting, they bring the food back into their mouths for a more careful chewing. This system helps the bison digest coarse grasses. It also helps them to squeeze more energy out of their food. Humans would starve to death on the bisons' diet of grass. Yet bison get enough nutrition from prairie plants to grow to be the heaviest land animals in North America. An adult bull may measure over 11 feet (330 cm) in length and weigh as much as one ton (900 kg) or more.

Most of that weight is packed onto the front of the bison. Its front legs are especially sturdy in order to support the hump over its shoulders. On the other hand, the bison's neck seems barely able to support its massive head. In fact, bison seldom go to the bother of raising their heads. Two-foot (60-cm)-long horns and a shaggy, unkempt coat that turns woolly in the winter make the bison one of the most easily recognized animals in the world.

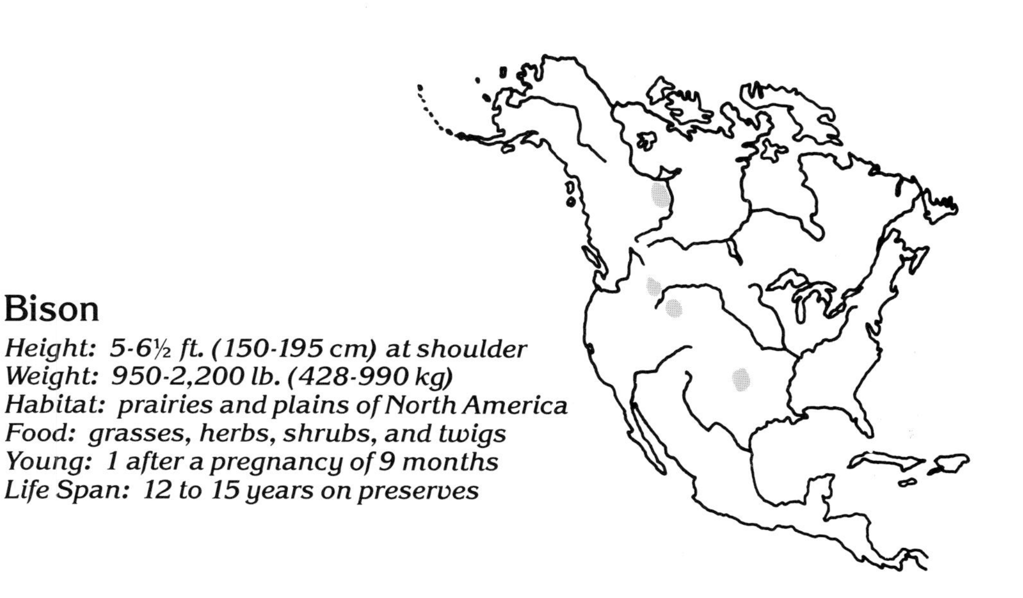

Bison

Height: 5-6½ ft. (150-195 cm) at shoulder
Weight: 950-2,200 lb. (428-990 kg)
Habitat: prairies and plains of North America
Food: grasses, herbs, shrubs, and twigs
Young: 1 after a pregnancy of 9 months
Life Span: 12 to 15 years on preserves

BIGHORN SHEEP

The nimble, horned animal that roams the mountains of North America is the bighorn sheep. About 40 inches (100 cm) at the shoulder, the bighorn sheep can be easily recognized by its massive, curling horns. Both males, or **rams**, and females, or **ewes**, grow horns. But it is the rams that wear the huge headpieces. These horns, which grow longer every autumn, can weigh up to 30 pounds (14 kg). That is as much as all the bones in the sheep's body.

Bighorn rams are famous for their mating battles. When two rams get ready to fight, they growl, kick at each other, and shake their horned heads. Then, like two gunfighters, they walk away in opposite directions. Suddenly, they rear up on their hind legs and charge at each other. Reaching a speed of up to 20 miles (32 km) per hour, they slam their heads together with a crash that can be heard miles away.

Few other animals could survive such a powerful head-on collision. But the bighorn sheep has two layers of bone over its skull that act as a crash helmet. After a few moments to steady himself, the ram is ready for another charge. Usually, the younger ram with the smaller horns gives up after a few head-knockings. But an evenly matched pair may keep bashing each other for hours.

These rams can give the same head butts to other animals, and so most leave them alone. The bighorn only needs to fear the cougar. However, bighorn sheep can escape these creatures by retreating to steep slopes. For safety, ewes pick their way onto narrow ledges to give birth. It is when the bighorns cross open valleys on the way to new feeding grounds that they are in great danger.

Even so, a bighorn sheep's senses are so sharp that it is rare when an animal can sneak up on it. Not only does the sheep have a keen sense of smell, its hearing is excellent and it can see clearly for up to five miles (8 km).

Bighorn sheep roam in herds, with the rams separate from the ewes and lambs for most of the year. The animals paw through the snow for plants such as juniper, fir, and sage. When the winter snows bury the plants too deeply for them to reach, the bighorn sheep move down to the lower mountain slopes, where the snow is not so deep.

Bighorn Sheep

Height: 40 in. (100 cm) at shoulder
Weight: 250-350 lb. (113-158 kg)
Habitat: mountains and forests of North America
Food: grasses, leaves, shoots, and twigs
Young: 1-4 after a pregnancy of 5-6 months
Life Span: up to 25 years in the wild

MUSK-OX

The musk-ox is probably the hairiest beast on earth. Its outer coat nearly touches the ground. The hair on that coat can grow longer than 30 inches (75 cm). Underneath the outer coat is a thick layer of wool called **qiviut**. In the spring, when the musk-ox no longer needs protection from the cold, this layer is shed. Each animal loses about six pounds (3 kg) of qiviut every spring. Qiviut is so valuable that some people have tried to tame the musk-ox herds so that they can collect and sell the wool.

Musk-oxen need their warm coats to survive in their frigid homelands. They live on the rocky tundra of North America and Greenland. Since few plants grow in this climate, musk-oxen must keep wandering to find food. During the short Arctic summers, they feed near lakes and streams on grass, flowers, and leaves. But the animals do not migrate to warmer lands during the barren winter months.

Instead, they move to high ground, where it is even colder! The musk-oxen put up with the icy wind because it keeps the ground swept free of deep drifts. It is easier for the musk-oxen to paw through the snow with their sharp-edged hooves to find the food they need. When a musk-ox finds a plant, it does not just chew off the top but pulls it up, roots and all.

Even for a very woolly beast, living in such frigid conditions can be dangerous. When calves are born, their fur is wet, and they can easily freeze to death if their mothers do not keep them warm.

Other than the weather, the musk-oxen's main enemy is the wolf. The musk-ox has developed an interesting battle plan. When enemies approach, the musk-oxen form a circle with the calves in the middle. In order to reach the helpless calves, the wolves must get past a solid wall of sharp, powerful, bow-shaped horns. Musk-oxen may weigh as much as 800 pounds (360 kg), and they are fierce and clever fighters. If they charged wildly at their enemies, their defensive wall would break up. So they take turns attacking, usually just one or two bulls at a time. They try to **gore**, or wound, their enemy with their pointed horns.

Like many other horned animals, the musk-ox's name is confusing. It is not really an ox, but is related to the mountain goat. The word **musk** describes the scent produced by glands in its face when the animal is scared.

Musk-ox

Height: 4-5 ft. (120-150 cm) at shoulder
Weight: 500-800 lb. (225-360 kg)
Habitat: tundra of the Arctic
Food: grasses, willows, and arctic flowers
Young: 1 after a pregnancy of 8 months
Life Span: 12-20 years in the wild

IBEX

The goat that walks on top of the mountains in Asia, Europe, and Africa is known as the ibex. Humans using the best mountain-climbing equipment struggle for days to reach dizzying heights of 16,000 feet (4,800 m). When they reach the top, they may find a Siberian ibex calmly picking its way among the rocks.

At such heights, even the ibexes' thick coats cannot protect them from icy winds, so they usually stay on slopes facing the sun. Female ibexes give birth during June and July, the only time of year when it is warm enough for newborn ibexes to survive.

Young ibexes, or **kids**, enjoy romping and playing. Adult ibexes, however, settle into a very quiet life. Their entire day is spent in eating grasses and shrubs, or by resting.

Ibexes eat even while they are resting. Like sheep, deer, and antelopes, the ibex chews a **cud**. In other words, it eats a lot of food quickly. Later, it brings the food back to its mouth for a more complete chewing. Scientists believe that grazing animals may do this for safety. If an animal can fill its stomach quickly, it will spend less time grazing with its head down, an open target for meat-eaters.

Not many enemies can follow the ibex to the mountaintops. But ibexes must move down to valleys in the middle of winter. There lynxes, snow leopards, and wolves will attack an ibex if they can find one.

The ridged horns of the ibex do not curl as much as the larger horns of the bighorn sheep. But they may grow to a length of five feet (150 cm) and can weigh up to 20 pounds (9 kg). This is quite a load for a 200-pound (90-kg) animal to carry on its head! The ibex grows a new section of horn each year, which makes it possible to tell an animal's age by counting the number of ridges.

The ibex has always been thought of as a lucky animal. However, the poor creature has had nothing but bad luck. People believed its horns could bring good health. They said its heart was a good luck charm and that other parts of its body could cure diseases. Because of this, some ibex species have almost died out. Other ibexes have trouble surviving because their ranges have been taken over by domestic sheep. In areas where they are protected by law, however, the number of ibexes is growing.

Ibex

Height: *26-41 in. (65-103 cm) at shoulder*
Weight: *200 lb. (90 kg)*
Habitat: *mountains of Europe, Asia, and Africa*
Food: *grasses, herbs, shrubs, and other plants*
Young: *1-2 after a pregnancy of 5-6 months*
Life Span: *up to 22 years in captivity*

GEMSBOK

For hundreds of years, people have told stories of a great horse with a single straight horn growing out of its head. This imaginary animal was called a **unicorn**. Although no one in the world has ever seen a unicorn, it is easy to see how someone could think that a gemsbok was one. When the gemsbok stands sideways, it looks as though only one horn is rising from the middle of its head.

The gemsbok is the largest, and perhaps most beautiful, of the long-horned family of antelopes known as **oryxes**. A male gemsbok may stand seven feet (210 cm) high at the shoulders and weigh 500 pounds (225 kg). His horns stretch three and one-half feet (105 cm). The female's horns are more slender but may reach four feet (120 cm) in length. These sharp horns may appear to be dangerous weapons, but the animals rarely injure each other with them.

Fights often break out among females as well as males when two herds meet at a water hole. Gemsboks do not stab each other, however. Instead, they lock horns and try to twist each other off balance. A cornered gemsbok will lower its horns to protect itself from any enemy. Even so, the horns seldom save it from its main enemy, the spotted hyena.

The gemsbok's majestic horns have made it a target of human hunters. Native tribesmen once killed the gemsbok in order to use its hide for shields and its horns for spears. More recently, the animal has been killed simply for its beautiful horns. Some types of oryxes, such as the Arabian oryx, have been nearly wiped out by greedy hunters.

Fortunately, the gemsbok lives in the rugged Kalahari Desert of South Africa where few humans ever go. Roaming in small bands of 2 to 12 animals, gemsboks are able to find food in places that look like wasteland. They use their hard hooves as shovels to dig for one of their favorite foods, the **chamma**. This large, melonlike fruit provides a healthy meal, and it is also loaded with precious water. Another way the gemsbok gets water in the barren desert is to lick the morning dew off plants. As the sun moves across the sky during the day, the gemsbok turns its body so that as little of it as possible faces the hot sun.

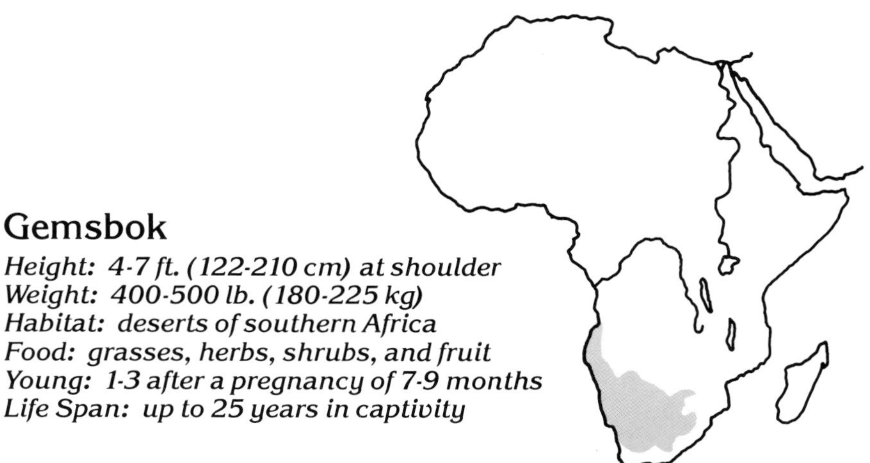

Gemsbok
Height: 4-7 ft. (122-210 cm) at shoulder
Weight: 400-500 lb. (180-225 kg)
Habitat: deserts of southern Africa
Food: grasses, herbs, shrubs, and fruit
Young: 1-3 after a pregnancy of 7-9 months
Life Span: up to 25 years in captivity

BLACKBUCK

The word **antelope** was first used to describe a small, deerlike animal that lives in India. This dark-skinned creature with corkscrew-shaped horns is known as the blackbuck. Along with its relatives, the gazelle, the springbok, and the impala, the blackbuck fits the description of the typical antelope. All of these slim-bodied creatures are capable of blazing speed, with springy legs and remarkable horns.

Among blackbucks, only males have horns, which grow as long as three feet (90 cm). Most blackbucks do not live up to their name, however, as females and younger males have light brown coats. As the males grow older, their coats darken with striking black-and-white markings.

Blackbucks are always on the lookout for enemies. If one animal senses danger, it warns the others by leaping straight into the air. All the blackbucks then run away with high hops and bounces.

At one time, the blackbuck was India's most popular game animal. Its beauty, its horns, and its speed made it an attractive catch. The blackbuck's speed turned the hunt into a kind of animal Olympics. Game hunters set up contests between two champion sprinters, the cheetah and the blackbuck. As fast as the 80-pound (36-kg) blackbuck could run, no animal in the world could outrun a cheetah. Fortunately for the blackbuck, cheetahs have become extinct in India.

Yet there were even greater problems for the blackbucks. More and more of the open areas where they lived became farmland. So blackbucks made themselves at home among the crops in the fields. Soon they made an enemy more dangerous than the cheetah. Farmers protected their grain by shooting blackbucks whenever they had the chance.

Not long ago, there were more blackbucks than any other hoofed animal in India. Now they are scarce. The few blackbucks that remain have been pushed to the desert areas where it is too dry to farm. Like many of their relatives, blackbucks can survive in a harsh environment. They eat plants that most animals cannot. Even in hot weather, they rarely need to drink water. Unlike many animals of the tropics, blackbucks do not try to avoid the hot midday sun. Instead, they feed during the day, right out in the open. Only on the very hottest days will the animals search for shade.

Blackbuck

Height: 32 in. (80 cm) at shoulder
Weight: 80 lb. (36 kg)
Habitat: grasslands of India
Food: grasses, leaves, and fruit
Young: 1-3 after a pregnancy of 6-8 months
Life Span: up to 20 years in captivity

DORNISCH

PRONGHORN

The pronghorn looks like an antelope and has often been called an antelope. But it is actually the only animal of its species. The name **pronghorn** comes from the hooked horns of the male. Females also grow horns, but their horns are rarely long enough develop prongs. Both females and males lose their horns and grow new ones each year, the only animal in the world to do this.

Native Americans called the pronghorn "the phantom of the prairie." It is the fastest running North American land animal. Two-day-old pronghorns can outrun a horse, but they cannot go that fast for long. Instead, they hide in the grass for three weeks until they are strong enough to run with the herd. Pronghorns seem to enjoy testing their speed, but they are not just sprinters. With large lungs and big hearts, pronghorns can run 45 miles (75 km) an hour for several miles.

The alert pronghorn has little trouble escaping from coyotes and bobcats. Only the very young are in danger. Out in the open plains, the pronghorn's large eyes can spot enemies long before they come close. While many animal mothers protect their children by staying close to them, female pronghorns do just the opposite, staying a quarter mile (.4 km) away from their young. They do this so that the little ones do not pick up any odor from their mothers, which might attract a hungry coyote. If an enemy comes near, the bucks try to lure it away from the does. In turn, the does try to lure it away from the young. As the pronghorns run, the white hairs on their rumps stand up as a signal to other pronghorns of the danger.

The pronghorn's coat is well suited to the change of seasons on the North American plains. The coarse hairs, which are about two inches (5 cm) long, lie flat in cold weather to keep in body heat. In warm weather, they stand up to allow the heat to escape.

At one time, at least 40 million pronghorns roamed the Great Plains. However, the animals have become much less common. Pronghorns like to migrate to better feeding grounds during the year, browsing for sagebrush, their favorite food. But the fences of ranchers stop them. Even though a pronghorn stands only three feet (90 cm) tall at the shoulders, it is able to leap as high as eight feet (240 cm). Yet it rarely tries to jump over a fence.

Pronghorn

Height: 36 in. (90 cm) at shoulder
Weight: 90-150 lb. (41-68 kg)
Habitat: grasslands of western North America
Food: shrubs and grasses
Young: 2 after a pregnancy of 8 months
Life Span: up to 7 years in captivity

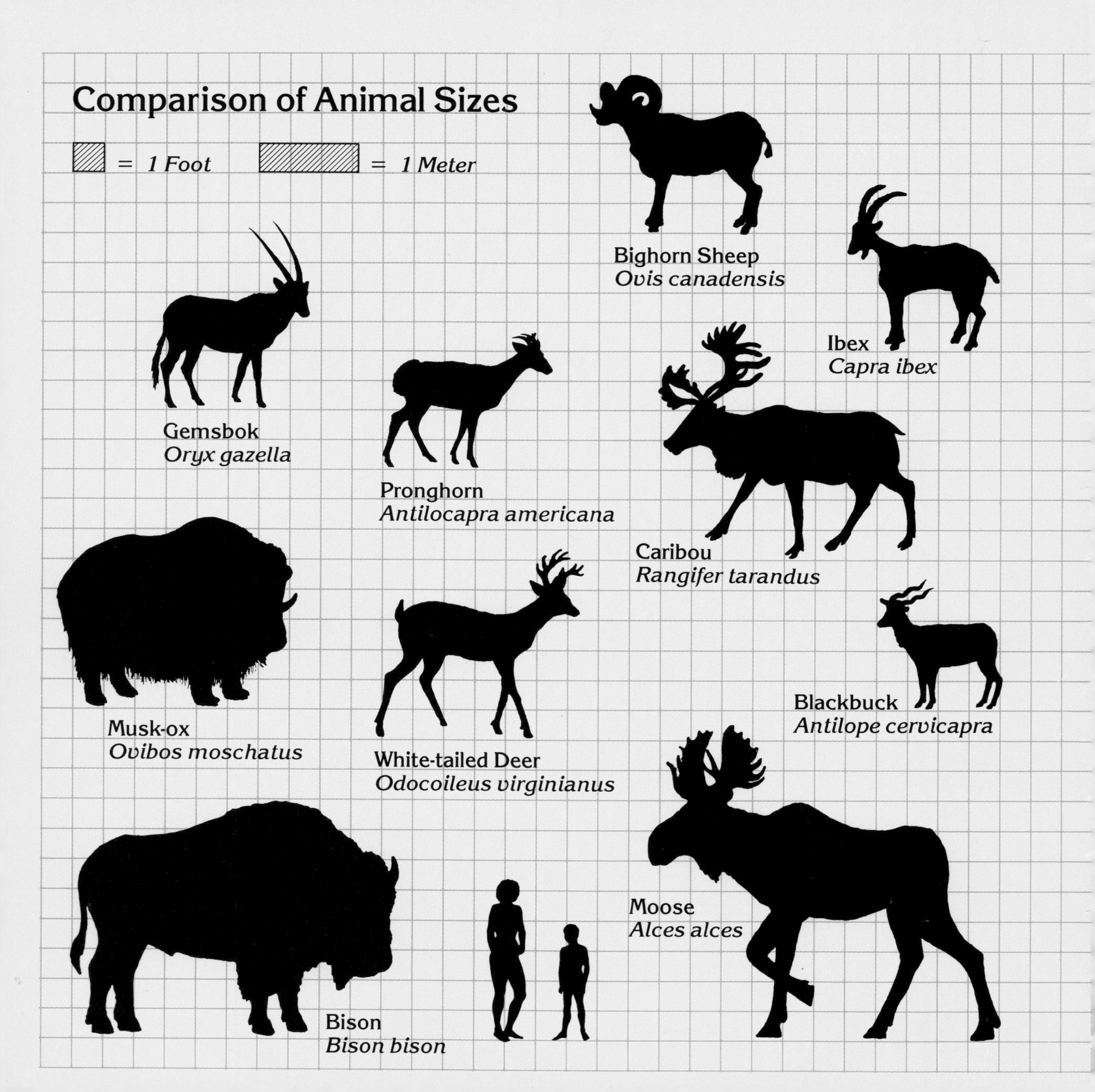
Comparison of Animal Sizes
= 1 Foot
= 1 Meter
Bighorn Sheep
Ovis canadensis
Ibex
Capra ibex
Gemsbok
Oryx gazella
Pronghorn
Antilocapra americana
Caribou
Rangifer tarandus
Musk-ox
Ovibos moschatus
White-tailed Deer
Odocoileus virginianus
Blackbuck
Antilope cervicapra
Moose
Alces alces
Bison
Bison bison